SELECTED POEMS

EDITED BY PETER FALLON

EILÉAN NÍ CHUILLEANÁIN

Selected Poems

WAKE FOREST UNIVERSITY PRESS

First North American edition published 2009

For permission to reproduce or
broadcast these poems, write to:
Wake Forest University Press
Post Office Box 7333
Winston-Salem, NC 27109

Cover design by Quemadura
Printed on acid-free, recycled paper
in the United States of America

LCCN 2008943055
ISBN 978-1-930630-44-4

First published by Gallery Press
Wake Forest University Press
www.wfu.edu/wfupress

Contents

for Macdara and Niall Woods

Lucina Schynning in Silence of the Nicht

Moon shining in silence of the night
The heaven being all full of stars
I was reading my book in a ruin
By a sour candle, without roast meat or music
Strong drink or a shield from the air
Blowing in the crazed window, and I felt
Moonlight on my head, clear after three days' rain.

I washed in cold water; it was orange, channelled down bogs
Dipped between cresses.
The bats flew through my room where I slept safely.
Sheep stared at me when I woke.

Behind me the waves of darkness lay, the plague
Of mice, plague of beetles
Crawling out of the spines of books,
Plague shadowing pale faces with clay
The disease of the moon gone astray.

In the desert I relaxed, amazed
As the mosaic beasts on the chapel floor
When Cromwell had departed, and they saw
The sky growing through the hole in the roof.

Sheepdogs embraced me; the grasshopper
Returned with lark and bee.
I looked down between hedges of high thorn and saw
The hare, absorbed, sitting still
In the middle of the track; I heard
Again the chirp of the stream running.

Ransom

The payment always has to be in kind;
Easy to forget, travelling in safety,
Until the demand comes in.

Do not think him unkind, but begin
To search for the stuff he will accept.
It is not made easy;
A salmon, a marten-skin, a cow's horn,
A live cricket. Ants have helped me
To sort the millet and barley grains.
I have washed bloodstains from the enchanted shirt.

I left home early
Walking up the stony bed
Of a shallow river, meaning to collect
The breast-feathers of thousands of little birds
To thatch a house and barn.
It was a fine morning, the fields
Spreading out on each side
At the beginning of a story,
Steam rising off the river.
I was unarmed, the only bird
A lark singing out of reach:
I looked forward to my journey.

Wash

Wash man out of the earth; shear off
The human shell.
Twenty feet down there's close cold earth
So clean.

Wash the man out of the woman:
The strange sweat from her skin, the ashes from her hair.
Stretch her to dry in the sun
The blue marks on her breast will fade.

Woman and world not yet
Clean as the cat
Leaping to the windowsill with a fish in her teeth;
Her flat curious eyes reflect the squalid room,
She begins to wash the water from the fish.

Swineherd

When all this is over, said the swineherd,
I mean to retire, where
Nobody will have heard about my special skills
And conversation is mainly about the weather.

I intend to learn how to make coffee, at least as well
As the Portuguese lay-sister in the kitchen
And polish the brass fenders every day.
I want to lie awake at night
Listening to cream crawling to the top of the jug
And the water lying soft in the cistern.

I want to see an orchard where the trees grow in straight
    lines
And the yellow fox finds shelter between the navy-blue
    trunks,
Where it gets dark early in summer
And the apple-blossom is allowed to wither on the bough.

Celibates

When the farmers burned the furze away
Where they had heedlessly lived till then
The hermits all made for the sea-shore,
Chose each a far safe hole beneath rocks,
Now more alone than even before.

Nights darker than thickest hawthorn-shade;
The March wind blew in cold off the sea.
They never again saw a sunrise
But watched the long sands glitter westwards.
Their bells cracked, their singing grew harsher.

In August a bee, strayed overboard
Down the high cliff, hummed along the strand.
Three hermits saw him on that long coast.
One spring the high tides stifled them all.

The Second Voyage

Odysseus rested on his oar and saw
The ruffled foreheads of the waves
Crocodiling and mincing past: he rammed
The oar between their jaws and looked down
In the simmering sea where scribbles of weed defined
Uncertain depth, and the slim fishes progressed
In fatal formation, and thought
                                If there was a single
Streak of decency in these waves now, they'd be ridged
Pocked and dented with the battering they've had,
And we could name them as Adam named the beasts,
Saluting a new one with dismay, or a notorious one
With admiration; they'd notice us passing
And rejoice at our shipwreck, but these
Have less character than sheep and need more patience.

I know what I'll do he said;
I'll park my ship in the crook of a long pier
(And I'll take you with me he said to the oar)
I'll face the rising ground and walk away
From tidal waters, up riverbeds
Where herons parcel out the miles of stream,
Over gaps in the hills, through warm
Silent valleys, and when I meet a farmer
Bold enough to look me in the eye
With 'where are you off to with that long
Winnowing fan over your shoulder?'
There I will stand still
And I'll plant you for a gatepost or a hitching-post
And leave you as a tidemark. I can go back
And organise my house then.
                                But the profound
Unfenced valleys of the ocean still held him;
He had only the oar to make them keep their distance;
The sea was still frying under the ship's side.

He considered the water-lilies, and thought about fountains
Spraying as wide as willows in empty squares,
The sugarstick of water clattering into the kettle,
The flat lakes bisecting the rushes. He remembered spiders
    and frogs
Housekeeping at the roadside in brown trickles floored
    with mud,
Horsetroughs, the black canal, pale swans at dark:
His face grew damp with tears that tasted
Like his own sweat or the insults of the sea.

The Apparition

The circular white sun
Leapt overhead and grew
Red as a rose, darkening slowly blue.
And the crowd wept, shivering,
Standing there in the cold.

The sharp-eyed girl miraculously
Cured by a beggar passed the word along.
Water, she said, and they found a spring
Where all before was dry.
They filled their jars with the water.

All will be forgiven, good and evil together.
You are all my children. Come back
In mist or snow, here it will be warm.
And forget the perishing cold,
The savage light of day.

Every Friday at noon the same;
The trains were full of people in the evenings
Going north with gallons of sour water.

Foreseeable Future

Not immediately, but
The day will arrive for my last communion
When I plan to swallow the universe like a raw egg.
After that there will be no more complaining.

Why did I wait so long?
You may well ask: the plan is such an old one,
Even as a baby I might have been sucking away:
I might have cut my teeth on it,
Nibbling off a bit every morning.
I was too modest and doubted my capacity
To consume it all singlehanded; I feared
Dying and leaving behind a half-chewed world.

So I was perfecting the stretch of my jaws,
Padding my teeth like the hammers of a grand piano
To save the works from shock;
Like the crocodile that ate the alarm-clock
I mean it to go on ticking.
This is going to be a successful swallow.
How could I have lived so long
If I had not known that day
Was bound to come in the end?

Family

Water has no memory
And you drown in it like a kind of absence.
It falls apart
In a continual death
A hundred-gallon tank as
Innocent as outer space.

Earth remembers
Facts about your relations;
Wood passes on patristic
Characteristics,
Bone and feather,
Scandal,
Charcoal remembering
And every stone recalls its quarry and the axe.

Lost Star

Starting from the window, the bars
And the three brick walls, the cherry tree
In the centre of the yard, most of its leaves
Lying light as feathers beneath, but some
Still clinging by twos and threes —
Not enough to shield the planet
Hanging there like a fruit

But further away than it seems —
Can I really see you swinging
Around me now in a circle
Whose radius is longer than the arms of any known clock?

The lonely pilot guides
The lost star, its passengers the crowd
Of innocents exiled in winter.
Sometimes, letting the vessel drift
Into danger, he pauses
To feed them at his miraculous breast.

Distant as the spirit imprisoned
In a bronze vase buried in shingle
At the clean edge of the sea,
Floating like instantaneous foam or an island,
Sealed off like a womb,

Here where I sit so still
I can see the milk in my glass is tidal
Inclining towards you across the dangerous sky.

Early Recollections

If I produce paralysis in verse
Where anger would be more suitable,
Could it be because my education
Left out the sight of death?
They never waked my aunt Nora in the front parlour;
Our cats hunted mice but never
Showed us what they killed.
I was born in the war but never noticed.
My aunt Nora is still in the best of health
And her best china has not been changed or broken.
Dust has not settled on it; I noticed it first
The same year that I saw
How the colours of stones change as water
Dries off them after rain.
I know how things begin to happen
But never expect an end.

Dearest,
          if I can never write 'goodbye'
On the torn final sheet, do not
Investigate my adult life but try
Where I started. My
Childhood gave me hope
And no warnings.
I discovered the habits of moss
That secretly freezes the stone,
Rust softly biting the hinges
To keep the door always open.
I became aware of truth
Like the tide helplessly rising and falling in one place.

Deaths and Engines

We came down above the houses
In a stiff curve, and
At the edge of Paris airport
Saw an empty tunnel
— The back half of a plane, black
On the snow, nobody near it,
Tubular, burnt-out and frozen.

When we faced again
The snow-white runways in the dark
No sound came over
The loudspeakers, except the sighs
Of the lonely pilot.

The cold of metal wings is contagious:
Soon you will need wings of your own,
Cornered in the angle where
Time and life like a knife and fork
Cross, and the lifeline in your palm
Breaks, and the curve of an aeroplane's track
Meets the straight skyline.

The images of relief:
Hospital pyjamas, screens round a bed
A man with a bloody face
Sitting up in bed, conversing cheerfully
Through cut lips:
These will fail you some time.

You will find yourself alone
Accelerating down a blind
Alley, too late to stop
And know how light your death is;

You will be scattered like wreckage,
The pieces every one a different shape
Will spin and lodge in the hearts
Of all who love you.

Letter to Pearse Hutchinson

I saw the islands in a ring all round me
And the twilight sea travelling past
Uneasy still. Lightning over Mount Gabriel:
At such a distance no sound of thunder.
The mackerel just taken
Battered the floor, and at my elbow
The waves disputed with the engine.
Equally grey, the headlands
Crept round the rim of the sea.

Going anywhere fast is a trap:
This water music ransacked my mind
And started it growing again in a new perspective
And like the sea that burrows and soaks
In the swamps and crevices beneath
Made a circle out of good and ill.

So I accepted all the sufferings of the poor,
The old maid and the old whore
And the bull trying to remember
What it was made him courageous
As life goes to ground in one of its caves,
And I accepted the way love
Poured down a cul-de-sac
Is never seen again.

There was plenty of time while the sea water
Nosed across the ruinous ocean floor
Inquiring for the ruinous door of the womb
And found the soul of Vercingetorix
Cramped in a jamjar
Who was starved to death in a dry cistern
In Rome in 46 BC.

Do not expect to feel so free on land.

I Saw the Islands in a Ring All Round Me

Far from the land, they had started to grow,
Far from complete, around the line of sky.
The boat edged across the circular bay
As loud as a circular saw
Slicing a wake through metal.
The sea expired in silence; the islands
Shuffled and swam. The circle
Edged slowly to the west.

The pilot is the pivot
In the middle of a clockface.
The boat slides evenly as the hand of a clock
Measuring time at the edge of the water.
She still recalls how his face
Against the primrose light, the curve of his forehead
Bisecting the horizon, cut off
An hour, the first horizon.

The Lady's Tower

Hollow my high tower leans
Back to the cliff; my thatch
Converses with spread sky,
Heronries. The grey wall
Slices downward and meets
A sliding flooded stream
Pebble-banked, small diving
Birds. Downstairs my cellars plumb.

Behind me shifting the oblique veins
Of the hill; my kitchen is damp,
Spiders shaded under brown vats.

I hear the stream change pace, glance from the stove
To see the punt is now floating freely
Bobs square-ended, the rope dead-level.

Opening the kitchen door
The quarry brambles miss my hair
Sprung so high their fruit wastes.

And up the tall stairs my bed is made
Even with a sycamore root
At my small square window.

All night I lie sheeted, my broom chases down treads
Delighted spirals of dust: the yellow duster glides
Over shelves, around knobs: bristle stroking flagstone
Dancing with the spiders around the kitchen in the dark
While cats climb the tower and the river fills
A spoonful of light on the cellar walls below.

The Absent Girl

The absent girl is
Conspicuous by her silence
Sitting at the courtroom window
Her cheek against the glass.

They pass her without a sound
And when they look for her face
Can only see the clock behind her skull;

Grey hair blinds her eyes
And night presses on the windowpanes,

She can feel the glass cold
But with no time for pain
Searches for a memory lost with muscle and blood —
She misses her ligaments and the marrow of her bones.

The clock chatters; with no beating heart
Lung or breast how can she tell the time?
Her skin is shadowed
Where once the early sunlight fell.

Old Roads

Missing from the map, the abandoned roads
Reach across the mountain, threading into
Clefts and valleys, shuffle between thick
Hedges of flowery thorn.
The grass flows into tracks of wheels,
Mowed evenly by the careful sheep;
Drenched, it guards the gaps of silence
Only trampled on the pattern day.

And if, an odd time, late
At night, a cart passes
Splashing in a burst stream, crunching bones,
The wavering candle hung by the shaft
Slaps light against a single gable
Catches a flat tombstone
Shaking a nervous beam as the hare passes.

Their arthritic fingers
Their stiffening grasp cannot
Hold long on the hillside —
Slowly the old roads lose their grip.

from *Site of Ambush*

3 STANDING MAN

The last bed excavated, the long minute hand
Upright on the hour,
The years in pain scored up are scattered and their tower
Down: time at a stand.

And upright on horizons of storm the monumental crosses,
Lone shafts like the spade
Haunting the furrow's end, flourish when man's unmade
Wedged in stones, sunk in mosses —

Aching an upright femur can feel the tough roots close
Gently over bone, stick
Fast holding a smooth shaft. Only the flesh such strict
Embraces knows.

6 VOYAGERS

Turn west now, turn away to sleep
And you are simultaneous with
Maelduin setting sail again
From the island of the white cat
To the high penitential rock
Of a spiked Donegal hermit —
With Odysseus crouching again
Inside a fish-smelling sealskin
Or Anticlus suffocating
Back in the wooden horse's womb
As he hears his wife's voice calling.

Turn westward, your face grows darker
You look sad entering your dream
Whose long currents yield return to none.

The New Atlantis

The feast of St John, Corpus Christi Sunday,
Houses breathing warmly out like stacks of hay,
Windows wide, the white and yellow Papal flags
Now drooped: one side of the street nods at the cool
Shadow opposite sloping towards the canal's
Green weed that reflects nothing. Turn a corner,
Nettles lap at a high hoarding, 'sites for sale',
Empty window-frames, corrugated iron
In the arches of doors, old green paint softly
Blistering on gates. Cross a lane: a kitchen
Bare, darkening with one shadow milk-bottle,
Then a bright basement — a bald man in his sleeves
Folding linen in a yellow room
                                        ... Whose lives
Bulge against me, as soft as plums in a bag
Sagging at summer. New Atlantis presses
Up from under that blunt horizon, angles
At windows like ivy, forces flags apart.

The Prisoner Thinks about the Stars

The outsides of stars
Are crusted, their light fretted
With dead bodies of moths.

And moving the sound they make
Sibilant stiff moth wings
Drowns the universal tuning-fork.

They sing like whales over the prisons,
They almost bump the roof.

Odysseus Meets the Ghosts of the Women

There also he saw
The celebrated women
And in death they looked askance;
He stood and faced them,
Shadows flocked by the dying ram
To sup the dark blood flowing at his heel
— His long sword fending them off,
Their whispering cold
Their transparent grey throats from the lifeblood.

He saw the daughters, wives
Mothers of heroes or upstanding kings
The longhaired goldbound women who had died
Of pestilence, famine, in slavery
And still queens but they did not know
His face, even Anticleia
His own mother. He asked her how she died
But she passed by his elbow, her eyes asleep.

The hunter still followed
Airy victims, and labour
Afflicted even here the cramped shoulders —
The habit of distress.

A hiss like thunder, all their voices
Broke on him; he fled
For the long ship, the evening sea,
Persephone's poplars
And her dark willow trees.

Night Journeys

There are more changes each time I return

Two widows are living together in the attic
Among the encyclopedias
And gold vestments.
                 A fishmonger
Opens his shop at the angle of the stairs.

The scullery I see has been extended,
A wide cloister, thatched, with swallows
Nesting over windows, now hides the garden.

I wake in Rome, and my brother, aged fifteen, meets me.
My father has sent him with a naggin of coffee and brandy,
which I drink on the platform.

And wake again in an afternoon bed
Grey light sloping from windowledge
To straw-seated armchair. I get up,
Walk down a silent corridor
To the kitchen. Twilight and a long scrubbed table,
The tap drips in an enamel basin
Containing peeled potatoes. A door half-open and
I can hear somebody snoring.

from *Cork*

I

The island, with its hooked
Clamps of bridges holding it down,
Its internal spirals
Packed, is tight as a ship
With a name in Greek or Russian on its tail:

As the river, flat and luminous
At its fullest, images the defences:
Ribbed quays and stacked rooves
Plain warehouse walls as high as churches
Insolent flights of steps,

Encamped within, the hurried exiles
Sheltering against the tide
A life in waiting,
Waking reach out for a door and find a banister,
Reach for a light and find their hands in water,
Their rooms all swamped by dreams.
In their angles the weeds
Flourish and fall in a week,
Their English falters and flies from them,
The floods invade them yearly.

3

A slot of air, the snug
Just wide enough for the door to open
And bang the knees of everyone inside;
You face a window blank with dust
Half-inch spiderwebs
Rounding the squares of glass
And a view on either hand of mirrors
Shining at each other in the gloom.

A woman's head, bowed,
A glint on her forehead
Obliquely seen leaning on the counter
At the end of a vista of glasses
And one damp towel.

And out of sight in the cellars
Spinning in the dust
The spiders are preparing for autumn.
They weave throughout the city:
Selecting the light for their traps,
They swell with darkness.

4

Missing from the scene
The many flat surfaces,
Undersides of doors, of doormats
Blank backs of wardrobes
The walls of tunnels in walls
Made by wires of bells, and the shadows of square spaces
Left high on kitchen walls
By the removal of those bells on their boards,

The returning minotaur pacing transparent
In the transparent maze cannot
Smell out his stall; the angles all move towards him,
No alcove to rest his horns.
At dawn he collapses in the garden where
The delicate wise slug is caressing
Ribbed undersides of blue cabbage leaves
While on top of them rain dances.

As the fog descends,
'What will I do in winter?', he thinks

Shocked by the echoing blows
Of logs unloading in courtyards
Close by, on every side.

6 A GENTLEMAN'S BEDROOM

Those long retreating shades,
A river of rooves inclining
In the valley side. Gables and stacks
And spires, with trees tucked between them:
All graveyard shapes
Viewed from his high windowpane.

A coffin-shaped looking-glass replies,
Soft light, polished, smooth as fur,
Blue of mown grass on a lawn,
With neckties crookedly doubled over it.

Opening the door, all walls point at once to the bed
Huge red silk in a quarter of the room
Knots drowning in deep mahogany
And uniform blue volumes shelved at hand.

And a desk calendar, a fountain-pen,
A weighty table-lighter in green marble,
A cigar-box, empty but dusted,
A framed young woman in a white dress
Indicate the future from the cold mantel.

The house sits silent,
The shiny linoleum
Would creak if you stepped on it.
Outside it is still raining
While the birds have begun to sing.

Séamus Murphy, Died October 2nd 1975

Walking in the graveyard, a maze
Of angels and families
The path coils like a shaving of wood
We stop to read the names.

In time they all come around
Again, the spearbearer, the spongebearer
Ladder and pillar
Scooped from shallow beds.

Carrying black clothes
Whiskey and ham for the wake
The city revolves
White peaks of churches clockwise lifting and falling.

The hill below the barracks
The sprouting sandstone walls go past
And as always you are facing the past
Finding below the old clockface

The long rambles of the spider
In the narrow bed of a saint
The names inscribed travelling
Into a winter of stone.

The Last Glimpse of Erin

The coastline, a swimmer's polished shoulder heaving
On the edge of sky: our eyes make it grow:
The last glimpse, low and smooth in the sea.

We face the air, all surfaces become
Sheer, one long line is growing
Like a spider's navel cord: the distance

From your low shoulder lost in the quilt,
An arm thrown forward: a swimmer: your head
Buried in a pillow like a wave.

The white light skirting the cloud pierces
Glass riddled with small scratches and creates
The depths and cadences of a spider's web.

A man is holding his baby and laughing,
He strokes her cheek with a brownstained finger
While his wife sews a wristbutton on his other hand.

The island trimmed with waves is lost in the sea,
The swimmer lost in his dream.

He Hangs in Shades the Orange Bright

So quiet the girl in the room
                           he says
It is a precarious bowl
Of piled white eggs on a high shelf

Against the dark wardrobe the gleam
Of skin and the damp hair inclining
Over her leaning shoulder fades
Into dark. She leans on a hand
Clutching the bedrail, her breasts pale
Askew as she stands looking left
Past the window towards the bright glass.
But from the window it is clear
That the dark glass reflects nothing;
Brilliance of the water-bottle
Spots the ceiling

The man in the courtyard waters the roots of the trees
And birds in their cages high on the red wall sing.

She moves her head and sees
The window tall on hinges
Each oblong tightly veiled. One side admits
Air through a grey slatted shutter, and light
Floats to the ceiling's
Profound white lake.

Still the sound of water and the stripe
Of blue sky and red wall,
Dark green leaves and fruit, one ripe orange
                                    she says
The sheet lightning over the mountains
As I drove over the quiet plain
Past the dark orange-groves.

March 18th 1977

Waking with a sore head
A freshly bruised shin,
Forgetting the collision:
Eyes open and see
With relief, my coat on a hanger.

The early light that slants
Warm from the curtain illuminates
The skin of your face,
Glittering all over like a lake in a light wind —
The eyelids, those fine
Horizontal folds: like cliffs by a lake
Layered and loaded with flowers.

When my skin was as smooth as
A jamjar of water
I looked for time in my father's eyes:
Brown and green circling,
A bead of yellow under the corner
When no part of my body
Was more private than a fish
Going round and round in a jamjar of water.

from *The Rose Geranium*

3

When she opened the egg the wise woman had given her,
she found inside some of her own hair and a tooth, still
bloody, from her own mouth.

One summer after another
The shore advanced and receded
As the boat shoved past the islands.

Dark bushy hills revolved in the path;
                             and in each
Of the solid still rooms above bars,
                         the first sight
Caught at an angle, the glass questioning your face.

4

'*A l'usage de M. et Mme van Gramberen*'
— the convent phrase (nothing is to be mine,
Everything ours) marks the small round enclosure,
Its table and bench. Distinguished
From the other old people, from the nuns' gravel
They sat in the windmill's afternoon shadow, half
Hidden by a moving carthorse's huge blond rump
And quarrelled over their sins for Saturday:
Examination of Conscience before Confession

Prepared and calm in case one thought
Struck them both, an attentive pose
Eluding me now, at ten in the morning, alone
With a clean college pantry: piled rings
Of glass rising, smooth as a weir.

The moment sways
Tall and soft as a poplar
Pointing into a lifetime of sky.

12

So rarely we lie
As then, in darkness
A vertical gleam relieved
Where the brilliance from outside
Struck the glass over the hearth

(Breast high, if one stood,
Night lapped the bookshelves
And a dying light floated
Above us, never reaching
Us, our arrested embrace)

I think at once of
That amphibious
Twilight, now that the year is
Revisiting the spring shrine.
At my window the sharp, grey

Rectangles of stone
Range, parade in squares.
February light
Spreading across the walls over my head
Washes my room with shadows, cold until morning.

15

Linked by precious chains
The feathered shapes moved with her as she moved,
Still descending lava stairs

Between scrub and a scatter
Of pines waving on the slope.
The command was, not to look
Down, but she did and saw the shore:

An oval sea, with the gleam
Of an iron lid raised an instant,
The rough pebbles where no boat rested
Or wave stirred among the weed.

And beyond the inlet, beyond the stiff black trees
That circle the burnt-out island,
Still flying, nesting, the slim grey birds
Without a cry, those birds of whom
No history of shapes transformed
Or grief outlived is ever told.
They flourish there, by the subterranean sea.

16

Because this is the age of his life
In retrospect he will name theirs
He calls now at noon to feed their cats;
And stretched on a chaise longue in the clean house
He bites one of the yellow sweet apples
Wrinkling in the dish, while the female
Noses his feet. The black cat watches him
From the padded rail at his elbow:
A short demanding stare;
                                        he recalls
A hand that shut off day,
An eye so close to what it sought, half-blinded,
A collage of hair and upholstery.

Beyond the half-drawn curtain, past the trailing boughs
Of their proper domain,
A goldfinch lights up
Childhood's cramped retreats,
Covenants made in
The scarce blood of berries
That dry on the twig.

The cats his shortlived witnesses.

17 AMELIA

Remembering her half-sister Amelia, that girl
Whose hips askew made every step seem upstairs
The woman at the airport tells me that from her
One spring she bought the first small car.

After that it was trains and taxis for Amelia
For years and years, while the younger lay
In the car in a leafy mews in Dublin
Making love to a bald actor
Her elbow tightening
Linked through the steering-wheel.

She tells me, this hot noisy afternoon,
That Amelia now drives a car like a cabin-cruiser
In Halifax, Nova Scotia, where her husband
Fishes for lobster in short ice-free summers.

18

I run my hand along the clean wood
And at once I am stroking the heads
Of everyone in the room.
                         Looking into the grain

Wavered and kinked like hairlines, what I see
Is the long currents of a pale ocean
Softly turning itself inside out.

Palm slack as air's belly touching the sea —
I feel the muscles tugging
In the wood, shoals hauling.

I look in vain for that boat
Biting its groove to the south-east,
For that storm, the knot of blindness
That left us thrashing
In steel corridors in the dark.

Beyond the open window
Along the silkpacked alleys of the souq
Momentary fountains and stairways
        (My hands move over the table
        Feeling the spines of fish and the keels)
I look, and fail, in the street
Searching for a man with hair like yours.

Pygmalion's Image

Not only her stone face, laid back staring in the ferns,
But everything the scoop of the valley contains begins to move
(And beyond the horizon the trucks beat the highway.)

A tree inflates gently on the curve of the hill;
An insect crashes on the carved eyelid;
Grass blows westward from the roots,
As the wind knifes under her skin and ruffles it like a book.

The crisp hair is real, wriggling like snakes; *like medusa*
A rustle of veins, tick of blood in the throat;
The lines of the face tangle and catch, and
A green leaf of language comes twisting out of her mouth.

The Pig-boy

It was his bag of tricks she wanted, surely not him:
The pipkin that sat on the flame, its emissions
Transporting her so she skipped from kitchen to kitchen
Sampling licks of food; she knew who had bacon
And who had porridge and tea. And she needed
The swoop of light from his torch
That wavered as she walked,
Booted, through the evening fair,
Catching the green flash of sheeps' eyes,
The glow of false teeth in the skull:

Its grotto light stroked oxters of arches
Bridges, lintels, probed cobbles of tunnels
Where the world shook itself inside out like a knitted
     sleeve:
Light on the frozen mesh, the fishbone curve, the threads
And weights.
                    And as day
Glittered on skin, she stood
In the hood of a nostril and saw
The ocean gleam of his eye.

Permafrost Woman

Now, that face he coursed
Beyond all the lapping
Voices, through linear deserts

Unfolds among peaks
Of frozen sea, the wave
Coiling upward its wrinkled grace.

Dumb cliffs tell their story, split and reveal
Fathomed straits. The body opens its locks.

Spying the crowded
Ocean graveyard, wrecks shifting
A sea mile to the west as the blow falls,

The traveller feels
His hair bend at the fresh weight
Of snow, the wind is an intimate fist

Brushing back strands: he stares at the wide mouth, packed
With grinding ash: the landslide of his first dream.

Street

He fell in love with the butcher's daughter
When he saw her passing by in her white trousers
Dangling a knife on a ring at her belt.
He stared at the dark shining drops on the paving-stones.

One day he followed her
Down the slanting lane at the back of the shambles.
A door stood half-open
And the stairs were brushed and clean,
Her shoes paired on the bottom step,
Each tread marked with the red crescent
Her bare heels left, fading to faintest at the top.

MacMoransbridge

Although the whole house creaks from their footsteps
The sisters, when he died,
Never hung up his dropped dressing-gown,
Took the ash from the grate, or opened his desk. His will,
Clearly marked, and left in the top drawer,
Is a litany of objects lost like itself.
The tarnished silver teapot, to be sold
And the money given to a niece for her music-lessons,
Is polished and used on Sundays. The rings and pendants
Devised by name to each dear sister are still
Tucked between silk scarves in his wardrobe, where he found
And hid them again, the day they buried his grandmother.
And his posthumous plan of slights and surprises
Has failed — though his bank account's frozen — to dam
    up time.

He had wanted it all to stop,
As he stopped moving between that room
With its diaries and letters posted abroad
And the cold office over the chemist's
Where he went to register deaths and births,

While the sisters went on as they do now, never
All resting at once — one of them would be
Boiling up mutton-shanks for broth, or washing out blankets,
Dipping her black clothes in boiled vitriol and oak-gall
(He used to see from his leafy window
Shoulders bobbing at the pump like pistons).
And still the youngest goes down at night to the stream,
Tending the salmon-nets at the weir,
And comes home to bed as the oldest of all
Can already be heard adding up small change with the servant.

London

At fifty, she misses the breast
That grew in her thirteenth year
And was removed last month. She misses
The small car she drove through the seaside town
And along cliffs for miles. In London
She will not take the tube, is afraid of taxis.

We choose a random bar. She sits by me,
Looking along the jacketed line of men's
Lunchtime backs, drinks her vermouth.
I see her eye slide to the left;
At the counter's end sits a high metal urn.

What are you staring at? That polished curve,
The glint wavering on steel, the features
Of our stranger neighbour distorted.
You can't see it from where you are.
When that streak of crooked light
Goes out, my life is over.

1981

River, with Boats

Of course she does not mind sleeping
On the deep fur of the bed
Beside the wide window
Where the birds hop,
Where the boats pass.

She can hear the hooters
Down there in a greeting;
She can see a flash of the river,
A glitter on the ceiling
When the wind blows
And the high branches of trees
On the other bank
Skip and bow in circles.

Only at the highest tide
The window is blocked
By the one framed eye
Of a tethered coaster
Swaying and tugging and flapping with the wind,
And the faces of the mariners
Crowd at the glass like fishes.

The Italian Kitchen

Time goes by the book laid open
On the long marble table: my work
In the kitchen your landlord painted yellow and white.
Beyond it the glass cupboard doors: behind them now
Ranged the green and yellow cups and plates
You bought in September and left behind, still in boxes.

One more of your suddenly furnished houses.
Eighteen years since we discovered, cash in hand,
Anonymous, the supermarket pleasures
Stacked and shinily wrapped, right
For this country, where all wipes clean,
Dries fast. Or California where you are now.

No sound from the man asleep upstairs.
At the hour's end I walk to the window
Looking over the slopes. Now the night mist
Rises off the vague plain, reaching
Our tall pine where cones cling like mussels:

Light still plays among the branches,
Touches the cold cheek of the windowpane.
I've bought blankets and firewood; we live here now.

To Eilís, Agello, March 1981

Quarant' Ore

At the dark early hour
When the open door of the church
Is pumping out light,
The sacristan is at work, unfolding
The stacked chairs, he carries them
Out of the porch, into the glow.
They spread wide like daisies,
They turn to the wide gold rose.
Follow it, ranked in rings.

And still it is not day
And the morning papers are lying
Dropped by gates in grey piles,
When the first pilgrims arrive,
Slipping into the dark shell of the porch,
To squat on the stone —
The practised knees doubled against the breastbone,
The elbows not interfering. They are packed
Lightly as drifted rubbish in corners.
They never obscure the blazing outline of the arch
Lying open for the real congregation
To roll up punctually in cars,
The knights with medals and white gloves.

A Voice

1

Having come this far, in response
To a woman's voice, a distant wailing,
Now he thinks he can distinguish words:
   You may come in —
   You are already in.

But the wall is thornbushes, crammed, barbed.
A human skeleton, warped in a dive, is clasped
In the grip of a flowery briar. His shrinking flesh
Reproves him, turns and flows
Backwards like a tide.

2

Knowing it now for a trick of the light
He marches forward, takes account of
True stones and mortared walls,
Downfaces the shimmer
And shakes to hear the voice humming again:

In the bed of the stream
She lies in her bones —
Wide bearing hips and square
Elbows. Around them lodged,
Gravegoods of horsehair and an ebony peg.

'What sort of ornament is this?
What sort of mutilation? Where's
The muscle that called up the sound,
The tug of hair and the turned cheek?'
The sign persists, in the ridged fingerbone

And he hears her voice, a wail of strings.

In Rome

The Pope's musketeers are breaking their fast
On the roof above my bed. Harsh burning of kebabs
Reeks down through the gap in the beams, and the retching
Of their caged doves. The captain lowered some charcoal
Last night; my poor girls are cooking eggs now
Behind the screen. Soon they must wrap
And veil up for the street, for the hours lounging
Nibbling bread in the Cardinal's front hall,
Twisting to keep their heels out of sight.

Then I have time to walk, alone on the carpet
On half the floor, where we eat and sleep together.
Not even the mice scramble on the clean boards.
We keep the bell-shrine there, and the gold chasubles
For the feast day. I must not go out.
But from the egg-shaped window
I can see the girls trailing back home, with a promise.

Indeed, only an hour after the markets close
The deaf runner from the palace climbs
With two silver pieces and odd coppers.
When we were at home it would have been three sheep —
Work for the troop, skinning, washing the guts,
Digging the pit for the fire. When the meat was eaten,
The wool to card and spin.
I am obliged to God for inventing the city,
To the Cardinal for the sound of money,
The clipped rounds, the battered profiles:
They circle my sleep like the faces of lost kin.

J'ai Mal à nos Dents

in memory of Anna Cullinane (Sister Mary Antony)

The Holy Father gave her leave
To return to her father's house
At seventy-eight years of age.

When young in the Franciscan house at Calais
She complained to the dentist, *I have a pain in our teeth*
— Her body dissolving out of her first mother,
Her five sisters aching at home.

Her brother listened to news
Five times in a morning on Radio Éireann
In Cork, as the Germans entered Calais.
Her name lay under the surface, he could not see her
Working all day with the sisters,
Stripping the hospital, loading the sick on lorries,
While Reverend Mother walked the wards and nourished them
With jugs of wine to hold their strength.
J'étais à moitié saoûle. It was done,
They lifted the old sisters on to the pig-cart
And the young walked out on the road to Desvres,
The wine still buzzing and the planes over their heads.

Je mangerai les pissenlits par les racines.
A year before she died she lost her French accent
Going home in her habit to care for her sister Nora
(*Une malade à soigner une malade*).
They handed her back her body,
Its voices and its death.

St Mary Magdalene Preaching at Marseilles

Now at the end of her life she is all hair —
A cataract flowing and freezing — and a voice
Breaking loose from the loose red hair,
The secret shroud of her skin:
A voice glittering in the wilderness.
She preaches in the city, she wanders
Late in the evening through shaded squares.

The hairs on the back of her wrists begin to lie down
And she breathes evenly, her elbows leaning
On a smooth wall. Down there in the piazza,
The boys are skimming on toy carts, warped
On their stomachs, like breathless fish.

She tucks her hair around her,
Looking beyond the game
To the suburban marshes.

Out there a shining traps the sun,
The waters are still clear,
Not a hook or a comma of ice
Holding them, the water-weeds
Lying collapsed like hair
At the turn of the tide;

They wait for the right time, then
Flip all together their thousands of sepia feet.

The Informant

Underneath the photograph
Of the old woman at her kitchen table
With a window beyond (fuchsias, a henhouse, the sea)
Are entered: her name and age, her late husband's occupation
(A gauger), her birthplace, not here
But in another parish, near the main road.
She is sitting with tea at her elbow
And her own fairy-cakes, baked that morning
For the young man who listens now to the tape
Of her voice changing, telling the story,
And hears himself asking,
Did you ever see it yourself?
                                      Once, I saw it.

Can you describe it? But the voice disappears
In a rising roar like a jet engine,
A tearing, a stitch of silence
Something has been lost;
The voice resumes
Quietly now:
                    'The locks
Forced upward, a shift of air
Pulled over the head. The face bent
And the eyes winced, like craning
To look in the core of a furnace.
The man unravelled
Back to a snag, a dark thread.'

Then what happens?
                          The person disappears.
For a time he stays close by and speaks
In a child's voice. He is not seen, and
You must leave food out for him, and be careful
Where you throw water after you wash your feet.

And then he is gone?
                    He's gone, after a while.

You find this more strange than the yearly miracle
Of the loaf turning into a child?
Well, that's natural, she says,
I often baked the bread for that myself.

Fireman's Lift

I was standing beside you looking up
Through the big tree of the cupola
Where the church splits wide open to admit
Celestial choirs, the fall-out of brightness.

The Virgin was spiralling to heaven,
Hauled up in stages. Past mist and shining,
Teams of angelic arms were heaving,
Supporting, crowding her, and we stepped

Back,[as the painter longed to
While his arm swept in the large strokes.]
We saw the work entire, and how the light

Melted and faded bodies so that
Loose feet and elbows and staring eyes
Floated in the wide stone petticoat
Clear and free as weeds.

This is what love sees, that angle:
The crick in the branch loaded with fruit,
A jaw defining itself, a shoulder yoked,

The back making itself a roof
The legs a bridge, the hands
A crane and a cradle.

Their heads bowed over to reflect on her
Fair face and hair so like their own
As she passed through their hands. We saw them
Lifting her, the pillars of their arms

(Her face a capital leaning into an arch)
As the muscles clung and shifted
For a final purchase together
Under her weight as she came to the edge of the cloud.

Parma 1963-Dublin 1994

The Architectural Metaphor

The guide in the flashing cap explains
The lie of the land.
The buildings of the convent, founded

Here, a good mile on the safe side of the border
Before the border was changed,
Are still partly a cloister.

This was the laundry. A mountain shadow steals
Through the room, shifts by piles of folded linen.
A radio whispers behind the wall:

*Since there is nothing that speaks as clearly
As music, no other voice that says
Hold me I'm going . . . so faintly,*

Now light scatters, a door opens, laughter breaks in,
A young girl barefoot, a man pushing her
Backwards against the hatch —

It flies up suddenly —
There lies the foundress, pale
In her funeral sheets, her face turned west

Searching for the rose-window. It shows her
What she never saw from any angle but this:
Weeds nested in the churchyard, catching the late sun,

Herself at fourteen stumbling downhill
And landing, and crouching to watch
The sly limbering of the bantam hen

Foraging between gravestones —

                        Help is at hand

Though out of reach:

                The world not dead after all.

1989

The Real Thing

The Book of Exits, miraculously copied
Here in this convent by an angel's hand,
Stands open on a lectern, grooved
Like the breast of a martyred deacon.

The bishop has ordered the windows bricked up on this side
Facing the fields beyond the city.
Lit by the glow from the cloister yard at noon
On Palm Sunday, Sister Custos
Exposes her major relic, the longest
Known fragment of the Brazen Serpent.

True stories wind and hang like this
Shuddering loop wreathed on a lapis lazuli
Frame. She says, this is the real thing.
She veils it again and locks up.
On the shelves behind her the treasures are lined.
The episcopal seal repeats every coil,
Stamped on all closures of each reliquary
Where the labels read: *Bones
Of Different Saints. Unknown.*

Her history is a blank sheet,
Her vows a folded paper locked like a well.
The torn end of the serpent
Tilts the lace edge of the veil.
The real thing, the one free foot kicking
Under the white sheet of history.

All for You

Once beyond the gate of the strange stableyard, we dismount.
The donkey walks on, straight in at a wide door
And sticks his head in a manger.

The great staircase of the hall slouches back,
Sprawling between warm wings. It is for you.
As the steps wind and warp
Among the vaults, their thick ribs part; the doors
Of guardroom, chapel, storeroom
Swing wide and the breath of ovens
Flows out, the rage of brushwood,
The roots torn out and butchered.

It is for you, the dry fragrance of tea-chests
The tins shining in ranks, the ten-pound jars
Rich with shrivelled fruit. Where better to lie down
And sleep, along the labelled shelves,
With the key still in your pocket?

The Water Journey

I sent the girl to the well.
She walked up the main road as far as Tell's Cross,
Turned left over the stile and up the hill path.
I stood at the door to watch her coming down,
Her eyes fixed on the level of the water
Cushioned in her palms, wavering
Like the circles of grain in wood.

She stepped neatly down on the road;
The lads on bicycles cheered as they passed her
And her fingers shook and nearly leaked and lost it.
She took her time for the last fifty yards
Bringing it to the threshold and there I drank.

I said to the other sisters, each of you
Will have to do the same when your day comes.
This one has finished her turn,
She can go home with her wages;
She would hardly make it as far
As the well at the world's end.

Passing Over in Silence

She never told what she saw in the wood;
There were no words for the stench,
The floated offal, the burnt patches.
She kept the secret of the woman lying
In darkness breathing hard,
A hooked foot holding her down.
She held her peace about the man who waited
Beside the lettered slab. He sang:

I went into the alehouse and called for a drink,
The girl behind the bar could not speak for tears,
The drops of beer flowed down the sides of the glass;
She wept to think of the pierced head,
The tears Our Saviour shed.

St Margaret of Cortona

Patroness of the Lock Hospital, Townsend Street, Dublin

She had become, the preacher hollows his voice,
A name not to be spoken, the answer
To the witty man's loose riddle, what's she
That's neither maiden, widow nor wife?

A pause opens its jaws
In the annual panegyric,
The word *whore* prowling silent
Up and down the long aisle.

Under the flourishing canopy
Where trios of angels mime the last trombone,
Behind the silver commas of the shrine,
In the mine of the altar her teeth listen and smile.

She is still here, she refuses
To be consumed. The weight of her bones
Burns down through the mountain.
Her death did not make her like this;

Her eyes were hollowed
By the bloody scene: the wounds
In the body of her child's father
Tumbled in a ditch. The door was locked,
The names flew and multiplied; she turned
Her back but the names clustered and hung
Out of her shoulderbones
Like children swinging from a father's arm,
Their tucked-up feet skimming over the ground.

Our Lady of Youghal

Flowing and veiling and peeled back, the tide
Washed the bulk of timber
Beached on the mud, so heavy
Twelve horses could not pull it.

A lay brother rose at dawn, and saw it moved,
The weight melted away,
To the shore below the water-gate.
He rolled it easily as far as the cloister.

At rest on the lip of weathered
Rough steps and the icy pavement,
It paused among the kneeling poor
The bark still crude and whole.

It takes the blind man's fingers
Blessing himself in the entry
To find the secret water treasured
In the tree's elbow; he washes his eyes and sees
A leaf cutting its way to the air
Inside a tower of leaves,
The virgin's almond shrine, its ivory lids parting
Behind lids of gold, bursting out of the wood.

No Loads/No Clothing/Allowed/in the Library

You must go naked in the library.
That pure white gown
They hand you entering weighs nothing at all.
You put it on, surrender
Everything but a few blank pages.
They lend you a pencil that writes and rubs clean.

The supervisor has long fair hair.
You sit underground,
She sees you on a screen, white against a window,
A marble court beyond. Her gaze sharpens,
A strand of her hair gets frozen, permanently
Trapped in the woollen band the man beside her weaves.

Just so twelve years ago I went to the church
With my hair hanging down,
I left my money and keys, I was driven
In a car not my own. There was trouble
When they led us aside to sign the papers —
They wouldn't write a line till they had their fees.

We could not move, our time settled in ice.
Sharp eyes watched in the crowd:
The beggar opened his bottle of *Marie Celeste*
And waved it around; my stepfather
Drew out a concealed cheque book; in the gallery
Over our heads the musicians sounded a retreat.

Home Town

The bus is late getting in to my home town.
I walk up the hill by the barracks,
Cutting through alleyways that jump at me.
They come bursting out of the walls
Just a minute before I began to feel them
Getting ready to arch and push. Here is the house.

Nobody who knows me knows where I am now.
I have a pocketful of gravel to wake my aunt sleeping
Behind the third dark window counting left over the bakery.
Here I will not be asked to repeat the story.
Between her and me and the hour of my birth
A broad stony stream is sliding
That changes its course with the floods of every spring.

Following

So she follows the trail of her father's coat through the fair
Shouldering past beasts packed solid as books,
And the dealing men nearly as slow to give way —
A block of a belly, a back like a mountain,
A shifting elbow like a plumber's bend —
When she catches a glimpse of a shirt-cuff, a handkerchief,
Then the hard brim of his hat, skimming along,

Until she is tracing light footsteps
Across the shivering bog by starlight,
The dead corpse risen from the wakehouse
Gliding before her in a white habit.
The ground is forested with gesturing trunks,
Hands of women dragging needles,
Half-choked heads in the water of cuttings,
Mouths that roar like the noise of the fair day.

She comes to where he is seated
With whiskey poured out in two glasses
In a library where the light is clean,
His clothes all finely laundered,
Ironed facings and linings.
The smooth foxed leaf has been hidden
In a forest of fine shufflings,
The square of white linen
That held three drops
Of her heart's blood is shelved
Between the gatherings
That go to make a book —
The crushed flowers among the pages crack
The spine open, push the bindings apart.

Woman Shoeing a Horse

This is the path to the stile
And this is where I would stand —
The place is all thick with weeds.

I could see the line of her back and the flash of her hair
As she came from the fields at a call,
And then ten minutes wasted, all quiet

But the horse in the open air clanking his feet
Until the fire was roaring and the work began,
And the clattering and dancing.

I could see by her shoulders how her breath shifted
In the burst of heat, and the wide gesture of her free arm
As she lifted the weight and clung

Around the hoof. The hammer notes were flying
All urgent with fire and speed, and precise
With a finicky catch at the end —

But the noise I could not hear was the shock of air
Crashing into her lungs, the depth
Of the gasp as she turned with a ready hand

As the heat from the fire drew up the chimney,
The flame pressing, brushing out the last thread,
Constantly revising itself upwards to a pure line.

I closed my eyes, not to see the rider as he left.
When I opened them again the sheep were inching forward,
A flock of starlings had darkened the sky.

Daniel Grose

The breach widens at every push,
The copingstone falls
To shatter the paved floor.
Then silence for three centuries
While a taste for ruins develops.

Now the military draughtsman
Is training his eye
On the upright of the tower,
Noting the doors that open on treetops;
He catches the light in the elder branches
Rooted in the parapet, captures
The way the pierced loop keeps exactly
The dimensions of the first wounding,
Holding in the same spasm the same long view
Of field and river, cottage and rock
All the way to the deconsecrated
Abbey of the Five Wounds.

Where is the human figure
He needs to show the scale
And all the time that's passed
And how different things are now?

No crowds engaged in rape or killing,
No marshalling of boy soldiers,
No cutting the hair of novices.
The old woman by the oak tree
Can be pressed into service
To occupy the foreground.
Her feet are warmed by drifting leaves.

He stands too far away
To hear what she is saying,
How she routinely measures

The verse called the midwife's curse
On all that catches her eye, naming
The scholar's index finger, the piper's hunch,
The squint, the rub, the itch of every trade.

Vierge Ouvrante

Overhead on the ladder
A craftsman can be heard ascending
Balancing the hammer and nails.

He tacks up the photographs:
How can he hold in his head all the leaves of that tree
Whose roots are everywhere, whose seed
Outnumbers the spawn of the ocean?

The woman in an anorak, snapped
Face down in a drain, her bare arse
Signalling to helicopters, hardly
Finds room beside the man boldly
Laid out on the stone slab
As naked as an elephant.

Mercifully in the last room
Cameras are not allowed.
You have to do your best with glass and shadows
And the light shining along the passages of your skull
To capture her, to remember

The opening virgin, her petticoats
Shelved like the poplars of an avenue
That slip aside until she uncovers the scars,
The marks of the ropes that chafed and held her
So she could not move or write but only commit
To the long band of memory that bound her like a silkworm's
   thread
The tearing, the long falling, the splashing and staining she
   saw.
And as she unwinds she begins to spin like a dancer against
   the clock
And in one minute the room is full of the stuff, sticky,

White as a blue-bleached sheet in the sun —
Till there is nothing left of the darkness you need
For the *camera obscura*,
Only the shining of the blank chronicle of thread.

Man Watching a Woman

The sound of everything folding into sleep,
A sense of being nowhere at all,
Set him on his way (traffic far off, and wind
In tall trees) to a back gate, a dark yard.
A path goes past the bins, the kitchen door,
Switches to a gravel walk by the windows
Lit softly above the privet hedge.
He stops and watches. He needs to see this:

A woman working late in the refectory,
Sewing a curtain, the lines of her face
Dropping into fatigue, severity, age,
The hair falling out of its clasp at her poll.
The hands are raised to thread the needle,
The tongue moves behind her lips.
He cannot see the feet or shoes, they are trapped
In toils of cloth. He is comforted.

He can move on, while the night combs out
Long rushing sounds into quiet,
On to the scene, the wide cafés —
Trombone music over polished tables.
He will watch the faces behind the bar, tired girls,
Their muscles bracing under breakers of music
And the weight of their balancing trays, drinks, ice
    and change.

The Pastoral Life

You remember how often we stopped
At that corner house to drink lemonade in the kitchen
And cycled on down to the harbour
The breeze filling our skirts.

But years later I passed their door,
Suddenly taking the mountain road.
I laboured up between rocks
Until when I turned east to the plain I heard

The corncrake in the shining grass.
The horses froze in troops of seven or eight
And a dull sound carried all that distance,
The bells around the necks of the leaders.

Will I ever go back? After the years I spent there
Depending on idleness that never let me down —
I waited for the wind to blow hairs in at my door
Carrying the story of the breed, for the right light
To show up the printing of muscle under the hide?
Could I go back after vesting my years

And leaving just once in November until the spring
When I found the plain blackened by fire
And staggered over bones too heavy for me to bury,

— Like finding a friend's ashes evenly shed
On the open page of a book?
                              I hear now, and believe it,
The grass has grown back
                    the horses are breeding there again.

The Party Wall

We were all still living at home then,
In the house with the fancy grilles
And the tall iron gates that let us out
Gliding to business and back at night for our tea.
We rose one morning to find the garden
Drifted and crisped with stiff white feathers.
They shone bluish against the red brick walls,
As they shifted and settled in the draught from the street.

We were not shocked at all until the next day
When the aerial photographs were published
Showing the house that backed against ours
But looked away across the Avenue
Visited the same, its roof and courtyards
Blessed with angeldown and cobalt shadows.

The tenants had my grandfather's name.
I went on my bicycle to see Father Deveney
In his room in the old priests' home.
We sat at the window looking towards Mount Desert
And he ate sweets and told me he remembered
When that house too had been part of his parish.
But he had never been told my aunt's story
About all the trouble over building the party wall.

That Summer

So what did she do that summer
When they were all out working?

If she moved she felt a soft rattle
That settled like a purseful of small change.
She staggered through the quiet of the house,
Leaned on a flowering doorpost
And went back inside from the glare
Feeling in her skirt pocket the skin on her hands,
Never so smooth since her fourteenth year.

One warm evening they were late;
She walked across the yard with a can,
Watered a geranium and kept on going
Till she came to the ridge looking over the valley
At the low stacked hills, the steep ground
Between that plunged like a funnel of sand.
She couldn't face back home, they came for her
As she stood watching the hills breathing out and in,
Their dialogue of hither and yon.

The Secret

Instead of burning the book or getting its value
They hid it and were silent, even at home,
So that the history of that lost year
Remained for each one her own delusion.
As the memory faded they had to live.
No one would buy their blood, but they sold
Their hair, the milk from their breasts,
Their signatures on slips of ravelled paper,
The grazing as far as the drawing-room windows
And at last the fresh fine grass
That had started to grow under the first arch
Of the bridge beside the burnt-out paper-mill.

A Witness

Can I be the only one alive
Able to remember those times?
What keeps them from asking the others?

As I start on my dinner of dogfish and cockles
A draught blows the hinges and one of them shuffles
In on the floor to sound me about our troubles.

Though he's nearly as old as myself the grey hags in the corner
Are beginning to watch his motions
As he loses his pencil and the page in his notebook.

I tell him about the day the mouse tumbled
In the one jar of oil and my mother shouting
At the Yank captain that all her geese were stolen.

I fix my eye on the mountain across the valley
Where we all came from and on the one cloud stalling
Clamped on the wild shelf, that will not move away.

Beyond the walls I can hear the children playing
In the riverbed. If I could tell what they are crying
It would lighten my darkness like knowing the language
   of birds.

A Hand, A Wood

1

After three days I have to wash —
I am prising you from under my nails
Reluctantly, as time will deface
The tracks, their branching sequence,
The skill of the left and the right hand.

Your script curls on the labels of jars,
Naming pulses in the kitchen press.
The dates you marked in the diary come and pass.

2

The wet leaves are blowing, the sparse
Ashes are lodged under the trees in the wood
Where we cannot go in this weather.
The stream is full and rattling,
The hunters are scattering shot —
The birds fly up and spread out.

I am wearing your shape
Like a light shirt of flame;
My hair is full of shadows.

Studying the Language

On Sundays I watch the hermits coming out of their holes
Into the light. Their cliff is as full as a hive.
They crowd together on warm shoulders of rock
Where the sun has been shining, their joints crackle.
They begin to talk after a while.
I listen to their accents, they are not all
From this island, not all old,
Not even, I think, all masculine.

They are so wise, they do not pretend to see me.
They drink from the scattered pools of melted snow:
I walk right by them and drink when they have done.
I can see the marks of chains around their feet.

I call this my work, these decades and stations —
Because, without these, I would be a stranger here.

Kilcash

from the Irish, c.1800

What will we do now for timber
With the last of the woods laid low —
No word of Kilcash nor its household,
Their bell is silenced now,
Where the lady lived with such honour,
No woman so heaped with praise,
Earls came across oceans to see her
And heard the sweet words of Mass.

It's the cause of my long affliction
To see your neat gates knocked down,
The long walks affording no shade now
And the avenue overgrown,
The fine house that kept out the weather,
Its people depressed and tamed;
And their names with the faithful departed,
The Bishop and Lady Iveagh!

The geese and the ducks' commotion,
The eagle's shout, are no more,
The roar of the bees gone silent,
Their wax and their honey store
Deserted. Now at evening
The musical birds are stilled
And the cuckoo is dumb in the treetops
That sang lullaby to the world.

Even the deer and the hunters
That follow the mountain way
Look down upon us with pity,
The house that was famed in its day;

The smooth wide lawn is all broken,
No shelter from wind and rain;
The paddock has turned to a dairy
Where the fine creatures grazed.

Mist hangs low on the branches
No sunlight can sweep aside,
Darkness falls among daylight
And the streams are all run dry;
No hazel, no holly or berry,
Bare naked rocks and cold;
The forest park is leafless
And all the game gone wild.

And now the worst of our troubles:
She has followed the prince of the Gaels —
He has borne off the gentle maiden,
Summoned to France and to Spain.
Her company laments her
That she fed with silver and gold:
One who never preyed on the people
But was the poor souls' friend.

My prayer to Mary and Jesus
She may come safe home to us here
To dancing and rejoicing
To fiddling and bonfire
That our ancestors' house will rise up,
Kilcash built up anew
And from now to the end of the story
May it never again be laid low.

The Crossroads

I have been at the crossroads now
All the time without leaving
Since the afternoon of Shrove Tuesday.

They brought me the blessed ashes
Wrapped in tissue paper.

When I woke on Palm Sunday
The palm branches had been left
On the damp stones of the stile.

I heard them at Easter
Across the ploughed fields,

And the little girls came and stood
A short way off, to show me
Their embroidered dancing costumes.

Now it is a long time to the Feast of the Assumption,
When my mother will come

To collect me in her pony and trap
And we will go calling on all our cousins
And take tea and sherry in their parlours.

Anchoress

In the last season, she changed her ways.
The pilgrim would find only
The mossgrown window beside the church porch
And through it at times a loaf and water were passed.

A few words, a command. Yes she knew who was there,
She still prayed for them all by name. I remember
When she would give me an hour of her visions,
When she would levitate — she was always deaf —
When thin pipe music resounded beyond the grilles.

The Angel in the Stone

Trampled in the causeway, the stone the builders passed over
Calls out: 'Bone of the ranked heights, from darkness
Where moss and spiders never venture.
You know what ways I plumbed, past what hard threshold;

'You see our affliction, you know
How we were made and how we decay. At hand
When the backbone splintered in the sea tide, you have heard
The twang of the waves breaking our bones.

'You look down where the high peaks are ranging,
You see them flickering like flames —
They are like a midge dancing at evening.

'Give me rest for one long day of mourning;
Let me lie on the stone bench above the tree-line
And drink water for one whole day.'

The Cloister of Bones

I begin from the highest point,
Best of all a belltower.

I see the tops of heads, cobbles,
Terraces all scuttling down
As if they hunted something buried
Between ledges where tables are set in the morning,
Under plants that grow over walls and pergolas,
The slopes of sheds, the stashed pruning-shears,
Under the measured walk of cats.

I am searching for a shape, a den, watching
For the cloistering blank of a street wall,
A dark reticence of windows
Banked over an inner court,
Especially rooves, arched and bouncing
Naves; a corseted apse,
And always, even if the chapel sinks
Deep inside, lit from a common well,
I search for hints of doors inside doors,
A built-in waiting about
Of thresholds and washed floors,
An avid presence demanding flowers and hush.

If I guess right I hope for
A runner of garden, the right length
For taking a prayerbook for a walk,
A small stitching of cemetery ground,
Strict festivals, an hour for the tremble
Of women's laughter, corners for mile-high panics:

And to find the meaning of the Women's Christmas.

Peace in the Mountains

The first day I saw this town
I came down the mountain road
Past the old border post, closed now.
The road-signs were in two languages
And the deer were feeding, away
On the far side of the valley,
Pausing and inching forward like photographers.
I slowed and paused and let the car slide forward
Again, the engine off and the gears loose,
Braking and pausing all the way
As far as the first houses and walled gardens.

The wind blew steadily, brushing
Every scrap of paper across the square.
There were rags of many colours
Bundled and packed on the trucks
In the railway siding. A gypsy woman lay
Where she had been struck down beside the bridge.
The ambulance stood by. The money changers
Had closed up their shops for the day.

The same as today, the rushing grey river
Tore downhill past the factory. Somewhere two streets away
It was Saturday and the immigrant weddings were feasted
Behind garden walls with sweet almond milk and loud music.

In Her Other House

In my other house all the books are lined on shelves
And may be taken down in a curious mood.
The postman arrives with letters to all the family,
The table is spread and cleared by invisible hands.

It is the dead who serve us, and I see
My father's glass and the bottle of sour stout at hand
Guarding his place (so I know it cannot be real;
The only boy with six sisters never learned

To set a table, though books lined up at his command).
In this room with a fire, books, a meal and a minute
When everyone is out of sight washing their hands,
A man comes through the door, shedding his coat;

He turns like a dancer before it touches the ground,
Retrieving a lily from somewhere. Where he has been,
You turn out your pockets every time a door is opened;
But the flower has travelled with him and he is in safe
      hands —

On the shelf a letter for him flashes a wide bright stamp.
He mutters once more, *Here goes, in the name of God* —
Women's voices sound outside, he breathes deeply and
      quickly
And returns to talk to the fire, smiling and warming his
      hands —
In this house there is no need to wait for the verdict of
      history
And each page lies open to the version of every other.

In Her Other Ireland

It's a small town. The wind blows past
The dunes, and sands the wide street.
The flagstones are wet, in places thick with glass,
Long claws of scattering light.
The names are lonely, the shutters blank —
No one's around when the wind blows.

The mistress of novices has sent all the novices
Upstairs into the choir to practise
The service for deliverance from storms and thunder.
Their light dapples the sharkskin windows,
The harmonium pants uphill,
The storm plucks riffs on the high tower.

And on the fair green the merry-go-round
Whistles and whirls. The old man has joined
His helper on the plinth. He calls his son
To throw him a rope, and watch for a loosening
Strut or a pelmet or the whole wheel
Spinning lifting and drifting and crashing.

But it spins away, grinding up speed,
Growling above the thunder. The rain
Has begun again; the old man's helper,
Darkfaced with a moustache, holds on.
They try to slow it with their weight,
Calling to the youngster to hang on the rope;

It's a small town, a small town;
Nowhere to go when the wind blows.

The Girl who Married the Reindeer

1

When she came to the finger-post
She turned right and walked as far as the mountains.

Patches of snow lay under the thorny bush
That was blue with sloes. She filled her pockets.
The sloes piled into the hollows of her skirt.
The sunset wind blew cold against her belly
And light shrank between the branches
While her feet shifted, bare,
While her hands raked in the hard fruit.

The reindeer halted before her and claimed the sloes.
She rode home on his back without speaking,
Holding her rolled-up skirt,
Her free hand grasping the wide antlers
To keep her steady on the long ride.

2

Thirteen months after she left home
She travelled hunched on the deck of a trader
Southwards to her sister's wedding.

Her eyes reflected acres of snow,
Her breasts were large from suckling,
There was salt in her hair.

They met her staggering on the quay;
They put her in a scented bath,
Found a silk dress, combed her hair out.

How could they let her go back to stay
In that cold house with that strange beast?
So the old queen said, the bridegroom's mother.

They slipped a powder in her drink,
So she forgot her child, her friend,
The snow and the sloe gin.

3

The reindeer died when his child was ten years old.
Naked in death his body was a man's,
Young, with an old man's face and scored with grief.

When the old woman felt his curse she sickened,
She lay in her tower bedroom and could not speak.
The young woman who had nursed her grandchildren
     nursed her.

In her witch time she could not loose her spells
Or the spells of time, though she groaned for power.
The nurse went downstairs to sit in the sun. She slept.
The child from the north was heard at the gate.

4

Led by the migrating swallows
The boy from the north stood in the archway
That looked into the courtyard where water fell,
His arm around the neck of his companion —
A wild reindeer staggered by sunlight.
His hair was bleached, his skin blistered.
He saw the woman in wide silk trousers

Come out of the door at the foot of the stair,
Sit on a cushion, and stretch her right hand for a hammer.
She hammered the dried broad beans one by one,
While the swallows timed her, swinging side to side:
The hard skin fell away, and the left hand
Tossed the bean into the big brass pot.
It would surely take her all day to do them all.
Her face did not change though she saw the child watching.

A light wind fled over them
As the witch died in the high tower.
She knew her child in that moment:
His body poured into her vision
Like a snake pouring over the ground,
Like a double-mouthed fountain of two nymphs,
The light groove scored on his chest
Like the meeting of two tidal roads, two oceans.

Translation

for the reburial of the Magdalenes

The soil frayed and sifted evens the score —
There are women here from every county,
Just as there were in the laundry.

White light blinded and bleached out
The high relief of a glance, where steam danced
Around stone drains and giggled and slipped across water.

Assist them now, ridges under the veil, shifting,
Searching for their parents, their names,
The edges of words grinding against nature,

As if, when water sank between the rotten teeth
Of soap, and every grasp seemed melted, one voice
Had begun, rising above the shuffle and hum

Until every pocket in her skull blared with the note —
Allow us now to hear it, sharp as an infant's cry
While the grass takes root, while the steam rises:

    Washed clean of idiom · the baked crust
    Of words that made my temporary name ·
    A parasite that grew in me · that spell
    Lifted · I lie in earth sifted to dust ·
    Let the bunched keys I bore slacken and fall ·
    I rise and forget · a cloud over my time.

Bessboro

This is what I inherit —
It was never my own life,
But a house's name I heard
And others heard as warning
Of what might happen a girl
Daring and caught by ill-luck:
A fragment of desolate
Fact, a hammer-note of fear —

But I never saw the place.
Now that I stand at the gate
And that time is so long gone
It is their absence that rains,
That stabs right into the seams
Of my big coat, settling
On my shoulder, in pointed
Needles, crowding the short day.

The white barred gate is closed,
The white fence tracks out of sight
Where the avenue goes, rain
Veils distance, dimming all sound,
And a halfdrawn lace of mist
Hides elements of the known:
Gables and high blind windows.
The story has moved away.

The rain darns into the grass,
Blown over the tidal lough
Past the isolated roof
And the tall trees in the park;
It gusts off to south and west;
Earth is secret as ever:
The blood that was sown here flowered
And all the seeds blew away.

Troubler

Did she know what she was at
When she slipped past the garden door
To palm the rolled notes from the teapot,

Or later that night when she pasted
The letter at the back of Hall's *Algebra*
And pierced the date with a needle?

So quickly the instant slid back
In the haystack, pressed by its fellows —
She spent the rest of the evening

Grinning on a sofa by the hour.
The photographs show her all flounces,
Engrossed, a glass in her hand,

But the others' eyes are like foxes' in torchlight;
She surely knew what she was starting: a ruffle
That probed like wind in a northern garden.

In her dreams it's not that she recalls them
But they come, the treasures of time
Lying packed like a knife in a garter

Or scattered among the leaves.
She hears the notes whistled on the half-landing
Just as the sweeping hand crowds the hour.

The Crevasse

He lay plunged in the funnel of a beanbag,
The glass in his hand as deep as a fjord.
The other went out to answer the telephone,

Leaving both doors open so he could see
A left leg, a left arm and half a ribcage
But no hand. On the far wall, glazed and framed,

A right shoulder and arm crushing flowers
Against a breast. He reached for the bottle again,
And all the vertical lines of the house moved

A little forward, and left. They dangled and waltzed,
Hanging brittle, ready to crash and split
Every straight chair in the room, leaving the halves

To hop away two-legged, leaving
The walls of the house wedged open
To the four winds and the polar light.

Autun

As I drove away from the sepulchre of Lazarus,
While the French cows looked sadly out
Under the wet branches of Berry,
I could hear other voices drowning
The Grande Polonaise on the radio:

Remember us, we have travelled as far
As Lazarus to Autun,
And have not we too been dead and in the grave
Many times now, how long at a stretch
Have we had no music but the skeleton tune
The bones make humming, the knuckles warning each other
To wait for the pause and then the long low note
The second and third fingers of the left hand
Hold down like a headstone.

How often was I taken apart,
The ribs opened like a liquor press,
And for decades I heard nothing from my shoulders —
My hair flying, at large like a comet —
How often reconstructed,
Wrapped and lagged in my flesh, and again
Mapped and logged, rolled up and put away
Safely, for ever.

On the mornings of my risings
I can hardly see in the steam.
But I know I arise like the infant
That dances out of the womb
Bursting with script,
The copious long lines,
The redundant questions of childhood.

She fills the ground and the sky
With ranked and shaken banners,
The scrolls of her nativity.
I stammer out music that echoes like hammers.

Crossing the Loire

I saluted the famous river as I do every year
Turning south as if the plough steered,
Kicking, at the start of a new furrow, my back
To the shady purple gardens with benches under plum trees
By the river that hunts between piers and sandbanks —

I began threading the long bridge, I bowed my head
And lifted my hands from the wheel for an instant of trust,
I faced the long rows of vines curving up the hillside
Lightly like feathers, and longer than the swallow's flight,
My road already traced before me in a dance

Of three nights and three days,
Of sidestepping hills and crescent lights blinding me
(If there was just a bar counter and ice and a glass, and a
    room upstairs:
But it rushed past me and how many early starts before
The morning when the looped passes descend to the ruined
    arch?)

She came rising up out of the water, her eyes were like
    sandbanks
The wrinkles in her forehead were like the flaws in the mist
(Maybe a long narrow boat with a man lying down
And a rod and line like a frond of hair dipping in the stream)
She was humming the song about the estuary, and the
    delights
Of the salt ocean, the lighthouse like a summons; and she
    told me:

The land will not go to that measure, it lasts, you'll see
How the earth widens and mountains are empty, only
With tracks that search and dip, from here to the city of Rome
Where the road gallops up to the dome as big as the sun.

You will see your sister going ahead of you
And she will not need to rest, but you must lie
In the dry air of your hotel where the traffic grinds before
    dawn,
The cello changing gear at the foot of the long hill,

And think of the story of the suitors on horseback
Getting ready to trample up the mountain of glass.

After Leopardi's Storm

The sky clears, and at the top of the street
I can hear the hen giving out her litany,
The stream rattling down the slope
In its tunnel of broom.
                              The lacemaker now
Stands at her window singing,
Her hand clutching her work, a cloudy ruffle
Wavering its fins in the watery breeze.

Her pale face like the sky
Slowly fills up with light, and spokes of light
Burst from the deep hooded clump of thunder, departing.

Reflected light lies about everywhere.
Like birds we approach, to sip and splash
At the edges of our watery nature, no more —

An ordinary festival that cannot be foreseen
Displays the original spindle
That never came loose, never turned,
But stayed until the long hours wrapped the stem,
Now dark, now bright, an overlapping of wonders
Each one confounding the last.

This afternoon salvation claims
Our whole attention, like grief,
Entirely here, on this side of the mountain
Where the single life is lived, the backbone
Upright, bracing for the next surprise.

Tower of Storms, Island of Tides

The founder of the lighthouse is not here.
She walks through other streets, pausing at a café
To smoke a cigar and check the news and the forecast.

She could not stay for ever in the blinding spray
Watching the sailors being blown on to the rocks,
Listening to the rain like a long thrill on the snare:

She paid for the pilot and the camera that photographed
The bones hanging on the cliff face on the one day of the year
That catches them in the northeast light between pleats of mist.

They flew on then to the islands further west
Where sandy shores offered a landing place:
One sheltered field, an empty house, salt pastures.

To live there would call for another skill, as fine
As judging the set of milk for cheese,
A belief in the wisdom of a long view from one window.

Water came swimming inward as the tide turned.
They saw far off a stranded dog rushing madly around
A dry patch of sand that was getting smaller and smaller.

It dashed off into the water, then back to its island
Which by now had almost disappeared.

The Bend in the Road

This is the place where the child
Felt sick in the car and they pulled over
And waited in the shadow of a house.
A tall tree like a cat's tail waited too.
They opened the windows and breathed
Easily, while nothing moved. Then he was better.

Over twelve years it has become the place
Where you were sick one day on the way to the lake.
You are taller now than us.
The tree is taller, the house is quite covered in
With green creeper, and the bend
In the road is as silent as ever it was on that day.

Piled high, wrapped lightly, like the one cumulus cloud
In a perfect sky, softly packed like the air,
Is all that went on in those years, the absences,
The faces never long absent from thought,
The bodies alive then and the airy space they took up
When we saw them wrapped and sealed by sickness
Guessing the piled weight of sleep
We knew they could not carry for long;
This is the place of their presence: in the tree, in the air.

The Horses of Meaning

Let their hooves print the next bit of the story:
Release them, roughmaned
From the dark stable where
They rolled their dark eyes, shifted and stamped —

Let them out, and follow the sound, a regular clattering
On the cobbles of the yard, a pouring round the corner
Into the big field, a booming canter.

Now see where they rampage,
And whether they are suddenly halted
At the check of the line westward
Where the train passes at dawn —

If they stare at land that looks white in patches
As if it were frayed to bone (the growing light
Will detail as a thickening of small white flowers),
Can this be the end of their flight?
The wind combs their long tails, their stalls are empty.

A Capitulary

Now in my sleep I can hear them beyond the wall,
A chapterhouse growl, gently continuous:
The sound the child heard, waking and dozing again
All the long night she was tucked up in the library
While her father told his story to the chaplain
And then repeated it before the bishop.

She heard his flat accent, always askew
Responding to the Maynooth semitones,
A pause, and then the whisper of the scribe
Sweeping up the Latin like dust before a brush,
Lining up the ablatives, a refined
Countrywoman's hiss, and the neuter scrape of the pen.

I feel the ticking of their voices and remember how
My sister before she was born listened for hours
To my mother practising scales on the cello;
A grumble of thick string, and then climbing
To a high note that lifted
    that lifted its head
        like a seal —
To a high note that lifted its head like a seal in the water.

Inheriting the Books

They've come and made their camp
Within sight, within slingshot range,
A circle of bulked shapes
Dark inside like wagons.
There are fires like open eyes.
I watch the billows of smoke,
The dark patches, hallucinating
Herds and horses.

Who is that in flashing garments
Bowing to the earth over and over,
Is it a woman or a child?
In the wedge of the valley by the stream
What food are they cooking, what names have they
For washing the dead, for the days of the week?

The long rope has landed, the loose siege hemming me.
In whatever time remains, I will not have the strength
   to depart.

At My Aunt Blánaid's Cremation

In the last dark sidechapel
The faces in the dome
Are bending down like nurses
Who lift, and fix, and straighten
The bed that's always waiting,
The last place you'll lie down.

But your face looks away now,
And we on your behalf
Recall how lights and voices
And bottles and wake glasses
Were lined up like the cousins
In a bleached photograph.

We carry this back to the city
Since the past is all we know —
We remember the snake called Patrick,
Warm in his Aran sleeves —
The past keeps warm, although
It knits up all our griefs:
A cold start in our lives.

Agnes Bernelle, 1923–1999

There is no beast I love better than the spider
That makes her own new centre every day
Catching brilliantly the light of autumn,

That judges the depth of the rosemary bush
And the slant of the sun on the brick wall
When she slings her veils and pinnacles.

She crouches on her knife edge, an ideogram combining
The word for *tools* with the word for *discipline*,
Ready for a lifetime of cold rehearsals;

Her presence is the syllable on the white wall,
The hooked shadow. Her children are everywhere,
Her strands as long as the railway-line in the desert

That shines one instant and the next is doused in dust.
If she could only sing she would be perfect, but
In everything else she reminds me of you.

Borders

for John McCarter

I am driving north to your wake, without a free hand.
I must start at the start, at the white page in my mind.
I no longer own a ribbed corset of rhymes;
I am the witch who stands one-legged, masking one eye.

Passed under the soldier's lenses at Aughnacloy,
I remember how often you crossed the map in a toil
Of love (like Lir's daughter driven to the Sea of Moyle
By spells) from Dublin to Portadown or Armagh
    to Donegal.

So I leap over lines that are set here to hold and plan
The great global waistline in sober monoglot bands,
I follow the road that follows the lie of the land,
Crossing a stream called *Fairy Water*, to come to the bridge
    at Strabane.

Gloss/Clós/Glas

Look at the scholar, he has still not gone to bed,
Raking the dictionaries, darting at locked presses,
Hunting for keys. He stacks the books to his oxter,
Walks across the room as stiff as a shelf.

His nightwork, to make the price of his release:
Two words, as opposite as *his* and *hers*
Which yet must be as close
As the word *clós* to its meaning in a Scots courtyard
Close to the spailpín ships, or as close as the note
On the uilleann pipe to the same note on the fiddle —
As close as the grain in the polished wood, as the finger
Bitten by the string, as the hairs of the bow
Bent by the repeated note —
                                    Two words
Closer to the bone than the words I was so proud of,
Embrace and *strict* to describe the twining of bone and flesh.

The rags of language are streaming like weathervanes,
Like weeds in water they turn with the tide, as he turns
Back and forth the looking-glass pages, the words
Pouring and slippery like the silk thighs of the tomcat
Pouring through the slit in the fence, lightly,
Until he reaches the language that has no word for *his*,
No word for *hers*, and is brought up sudden
Like a boy in a story faced with a small locked door.
Who is that he can hear panting on the other side?
The steam of her breath is turning the locked lock green.